101 Tips
Residen

MW01249219

101 Tips to Getting the Residency You Want

A Guide for Medical Students

John Canady, MD

University of Iowa Press, Iowa City

University of Iowa Press, Iowa City 52242

Copyright © 2008 by the University of Iowa Press

www.uiowapress.org

Printed in the United States of America

Design by April Leidig-Higgins

The University of Iowa Press is a member of Green Press
Initiative and is committed to preserving natural resources.

Printed on acid-free paper

Library of Congress Cataloging-in-Publication Data

Canady, John, 1957–

101 tips to getting the residency you want: a guide for
    medical students / John Canady.

p.   ; cm.

ISBN-13: 978-1-58729-682-6 (pbk)

ISBN-10: 1-58729-682-9 (pbk)

    1. Medicine—Study and teaching (Residency)—United
States.   2. Medicine—Vocational guidance—United
States.   I. Title.   II. Title: One hundred one tips to getting
the residency you want.

    [DNLM: 1. Internship and Residency.   2. Students, Medical.
3. Vocational Guidance.   W 20 C21270 2008]

R840.C35 2008

610.71'173—dc22   2008011497

08 09 10 11 12 P 5 4 3 2 1

Contents

Introduction

This book was born out of a need to help junior and senior medical students get the residencies they want. For a number of years I have served both as an advisor to individual students at the University of Iowa and as the faculty advisor to a group of students interested in careers in surgical disciplines, the Iowa Surgical Interest Society. Once a year, this group has a meeting where a panel of senior medical students graciously gives a couple of hours of its time and lets the M1s (first-year students), M2s (second-year students), and M3s (third-year students) in the group ask any question they like about the residency application process.

I am convinced that these sessions are invaluable to those students who have yet to begin the residency application process. This book is a compilation of some of the best tips, tricks, and tactics that have come out of these meetings. Also included are some of the pearls I have learned during my academic career. Used properly, they will provide you with an advantage that may help you get the residency you want. Good luck.

Thoughts for a Good Start

The tips that follow may seem rather basic but that is actually a good thing because it probably means you have already thought through the points being made and you are in a very good place to begin the process of getting the residency you want. The main concepts are to know yourself and do what you want to do, to make things as easy on yourself outside of your residency as you can, and to realize that your residency is really connected to the rest of your life. So make the most of it every way you can.

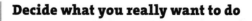

Decide what you really want to do

This may seem obvious, but you would be surprised how many residents end up in careers because their parents were that type of physician or they see some other potential practice opportunity beckoning when they are done. Circumstances change, people change, opportunities change, and the only way to know that you will be happy is to pick a field that you really want to be in. When you are doing something you want to do, it is easy to do it well.

In medical school the first question you should try to ask yourself is whether you want to practice medicine or surgery. This is a very basic distinction that, once made, will greatly simplify your senior schedule and residency application. If you are good with your hands, you like to fix things, and you like quick results, you may be leaning toward a surgical or procedurally based career. If you like managing problems over a longer period of time or enjoy seeing patients in your practice for a number of years, you may be better suited for a cognitive career in internal medicine, pediatrics, or family practice. Of course, even after you have made this choice, there are still more decisions to make regarding subspecialties within any of these broad areas.

Decide where you want to live during your residency

You are not going to have a lot of time to enjoy all that an area has to offer during the training programs in most residencies. That said, you will have some free time and if there is a part of the country where you have always wanted to live, now is your chance to try it out. A more practical concern for a resident, though, is how easy it is going to be for you to get back and forth to work, how expensive housing is, and how easy it is to access the necessities of daily living, such as grocery stores, laundromats, and cleaners. If you have a family, you will also need to think about job opportunities for your spouse, schools for your kids, safety for your family, kennels for the pets, and so forth.

Decide where you want to live after your residency

This is often overlooked in the residency selection process, but it is not uncommon to find yourself practicing in the area of the country where you did your residency. The reasons for this are that you will have the opportunity to meet local and regional physicians in your specialty during your training, and these acquaintances may turn into job offers when you finish training. Certainly you can leave your residency and go anywhere you want when you are done, but you may have the opportunity to get a foot in the door in the local area around your training program. Training in a given geographical area may give you the inside track toward job opportunities that are not widely advertised.

Decide how you want to live during your residency

By this point in your life you know that there are multiple housing options available in any town or city at a range of prices. How much you are able to pay for housing will depend on your resident stipend, your debt load from college and medical school, and your family situation. Keep in mind that you will have little free time during most residencies, and you may want to spend that time doing things you enjoy rather than using the time doing repairs or maintenance to the place you live. The housing you have during your residency is a temporary situation. You need to have the flexibility to devote yourself to your training and not be consumed by problems with your house or apartment.

Making Connections

- -

The tips in this section are really what getting a residency is all about. The personal connections you make, not the forms you fill out, will make you successful. If there is any way to schedule an out-of-town rotation in your specialty, you should do it.

Pick out-of-town rotations carefully

Your out-of-town rotations should fall into one or two of three groups: programs you are reasonably competitive for and really like, programs that are very well thought of, or programs that you feel you might have a leg up on getting into because of some *intangibles* in the process. The latter group will be more extensively discussed later, but this group would include programs that a family member or close friend may have completed or you feel you have some other special "in." Any other use of out-of-town rotations is, in my opinion, a waste of your time.

A classical example of this is the *geographic and meteorological* method of selecting a rotation at a program to take full advantage of skiing, surfing, diving, or some other recreational activity. Unless you are truly an outstanding candidate, you cannot afford to waste time in these pursuits at this time in your life. Save it for later when you can really enjoy it.

Use the "Good Ol' Boy or Girl" network as much as you can

This may sound a bit old-fashioned, but the reality is that people (both men and women) talk to each other and this can work either for or against you. Don't be afraid to use networks and contacts that are available to you. If someone is willing to put in a good word for you at a program and can do it in a way that is not overbearing or offensive, then by all means, have them do it. This is not cheating. This is using the resources available to you in the most effective fashion. This is exactly what everyone else you are competing against will be doing.

7 An advance letter or e-mail is ten times better than just showing up

If you are able to have someone from your home institution vouch for you before you show up for an away rotation, you will definitely have an advantage from the start. Formal letters of introduction may be a thing of the past in most circumstances, but the icebreaking effect that a letter or e-mail may have for you should not be underestimated. You only have one chance to make a first impression and having someone help shape that first impression with a letter or e-mail before you are even there could be a big help.

8 An advance phone call is ten times better than any letter

This is true for at least two reasons. People will tend to call other people when they know them better so a phone call is likely to have more influence than a letter because of the closer relationship it implies. Also, more emotion and information can be transmitted in just a few minutes on the phone than can be done with a letter. If one of your staff offers to call on your behalf, you should take them up on the offer. If you know them well enough and they don't offer, you might consider asking them to do so. Again, this can help you make a superb first impression and get off to a great start at your elective rotation.

9 The only question you should ask yourself during your elective outside rotations is "Can I be doing more?"

Elective out-of-town rotations can be a great time to see a new part of the country, explore a new city, or just catch your breath from what is going on at home. However, if you make any of these a priority during your away rotations, you are probably not maximizing your chances of getting into that program. Remember that everyone likes a party and everyone likes a party guy/gal, but not everyone wants to hire one as a resi-dent. Your main goal during your relatively short time at the away rotation should be to impress everyone you can by showing them that no one they have ever had as a rotating medical student has worked harder or wanted a spot in that program more. Get there early and stay late. Read like crazy and offer to do presenta-tions if appropriate. Don't stop working until you get on the plane or in the car to go home.

Use the out-of-town faculty as references

When you have finished your elective rotation, don't be afraid to use the out-of-town faculty as references if you have made a good impression and hit it off well with them. Again, this serves to further expand your network because the faculty in a different program may have different friends and contacts than those who are available to you at your home institution. Of course, working hard at your out-of-town rotation is a prerequisite for getting this kind of help from faculty who only have a few weeks to get to know you.

Select the programs you apply to with a careful plan

Here's a strategy I commonly suggest for arriving at a reasonable number of programs for your application process:

A. Ask your local *staff* which programs they think are the best and if they think there are any good "sleeper" programs out there where your odds of acceptance might be higher than in the more competitive programs. The staff can provide a long-term perspective of how programs have stacked up over time, what trends they are seeing at meetings, and how national and regional politics within the specialty are likely to impact specific individuals and programs. However, it is important to realize that some of this information may be out of date or not entirely accurate. Unless a particular faculty person has just been a visiting professor at a given institution or has close personal contacts there, they may not know what is actually going on at another program right now. So the information you will get from them will have a good historical view, but important things may have recently changed at a program and your staff may not be aware of this.

B. Next, ask the *chief residents* at your home program for a list of which programs they think are the best. These people will have the benefit of being just about to complete a training program and have probably been to a national meeting or two to talk to other residents about their experience with other programs. This group of recommendations will somewhat blend the long-term view of the staff recommendations with the short-term perspective of residents. Compared to the more junior residents, the senior residents will have a more refined sense of what is truly important in a training program and which training programs are currently strong.

C. Finally, ask the *most junior residents* in the specialty you are considering what their favorite programs were from their recent interview trips. Listen carefully to what they tell you, but take some of the information with a grain of salt. This group will likely have the most up-to-date information on what is going on at specific programs, but will lack some of the perspective on what it all means. Nonetheless, they are a prime source of information about what is really and truly going on at the present time in the programs where they just interviewed.

After you have the lists of programs from all three of these groups, take some time to sift through them and find the similarities. It is certainly not necessary for all three of these groups to recommend a program for it to be a good choice. However, if the program is recommended by all three groups, you can pretty well rest assured that it is a solid program with a long-term reputation and no recent skeletons in the closet.

12 Don't forget legacy private-practice physicians you might know or those who may have been your treating physicians

In your efforts to get letters of recommendation and phone calls on your behalf, don't overlook physicians in private practice in the specialty you are seeking. While it is certainly true that academic physicians network with each other and like to produce more of themselves, it is also common for very good residents to go into private practice. This is true even in programs that have national reputations for turning out academic doctors. Recommendations from carefully selected graduates such as these can hold tremendous weight with staff that still remember them from their training.

13

Get to know the chief of the program as much as possible, both in your home institution and on your away rotations

This is not a blatant recommendation to engage in brownnosing of the department chair. A simple fact of life is that the chief of the division or department will have a great deal of say in who the residents are in the program. This influence may be done in a public way or done privately, but you can be sure this will be done to some extent in virtually every program in every specialty.

A chief knows that he or she will eventually recommend the people selected for the program and the chief also knows that he or she will ultimately be responsible if one of the residents gets into trouble. The point of this tip is to simply recognize this as a fact of life and deal with it as best you can. The better the chief of a program likes you, the more likely you are to get in. Period.

14

Get to know the other faculty as much as possible, but be aware of factions within the department

Of course, the previous tip is not an invitation to snub the other faculty in a program. Developing a broad base of support is important and will improve your chances of getting a slot in the program. You will not be doing yourself any favors if you work exclusively with the chief. This is especially important if your interests, research, or future plans lie in a subspecialty area that is not the chief's interest. In cases like this, you are probably best served to get to know the chief of the service and also to spend time with a senior faculty person who has a practice or research area that focuses on what you are interested in.

You also need to understand that within almost every academic department, there are factions and politics working on agendas that you should have no part of. Be sensitive to the existence of these kinds of things and stay away from intradepartmental politics. Don't let yourself get used as a pawn, especially against the departmental chief.

15 Be nice to the administrative assistants because they may have a vote (and even if they don't, they will still have their say)

There's an old saying that if you want to know how your fiancé will treat you after you are married, you should take him out to dinner and watch the way he treats the waiter. The analogy to this saying in picking residents is to watch how the applicants treat the administrative assistants. Sometimes the behavior the administrative assistants report is almost unbelievable. However, after hearing the same stories for so many years of interviewing residency candidates, I have to believe them. I believe the stories because I know that the truth about how some of the applicants acted is a whole lot worse than anything the administrative assistants would have made up.

For the record, I have been involved with residency selection in programs where the administrative assistants as a group got a vote equal to a faculty member's vote. Now this is not to say that the administrative assistants had an equal number of votes to the staff, but if they were determined to blackball someone, the staff rarely voted against their opinion. The administrative assistants didn't do this very often, but when they did, the resident applicant didn't have a chance. If you are a faculty person in a competitive program, the choice between making the administrative assistants angry by picking a resident candidate they don't like or just moving on to another applicant is a no-brainer.

Therefore, you should be nice to *everyone* you meet in the department during your interview. This certainly seems to be common sense, but common sense is not always as common as one may think. If you get into an argument with one of the administrative assistants, you are going to lose no matter whose fault the problem really is. The best way to avoid this is to go out of your way to make sure your application is complete and handed in on time, and that you have communicated with the appropriate people far enough ahead of the deadlines to fix problems without undue stress.

Just a note about going too far, though. Gratuitous sucking up is almost as offensive as arrogant and rude behavior, so don't go overboard.

16

If possible, talk to people who have recently graduated from the program

This could be easy if some of your local staff are recent graduates of the program you are considering. There may also be physicians in private practice in your area who have recently graduated from the program. A phone call to them to get their impression would be worthwhile, and they will almost always be happy to talk to you for a few minutes about their training program. An important aspect of this information is that they will be able to give you some insight on how well the program prepared them for actual practice.

17

Contact students who have recently graduated and are in the city where you are interviewing

Keep in touch with students in classes ahead of you after they have left for their residency spots, especially if they are in a program or town where you might like to interview. Not only can they be an excellent source of information about the town and/or program, but they also may have space where you could spend the night while you are there interviewing. Don't be shy about asking them if you can stay with them. Most residents don't have a lot of time, but they do remember that the interviewing process was tough, and in most cases they will be happy to help out. This also gives them a chance to catch up on what is going on back at their old medical school. If you are given a free place to stay, a nice touch is offering to buy something inexpensive for dinner, like a pizza or some Chinese food. Residents will hardly ever turn down a meal that they do not have to cook.

18 Use your time at an away location to learn something about the city the training program is located in

Initially, this advice may seem at odds with previous thoughts about working all you can to make a good impression during your time at the away rotation. However, it really isn't. You should be tireless at work, but even if you do that, you will still have some time to look around the town a little. Get some real-estate flyers and get a feel for where you might possibly live if you trained there and what the cost of living might be. Use your weekend time to tour the city a little bit and get a feel for the parts of town away from the nightlife. If things are going really well with your rotation, you might even want to have a preliminary talk with some realtors, and let them know what you are interested in so that if something becomes available after you leave, they can contact you to see if you are interested. Generally speaking, if you are going to be at a location between two and three years or less, most experts recommend not buying a house. On the other hand, there are sweet deals that pop up in every city. If you do decide to buy, remember the first law of real estate: location, location, location. If the location of the house is attractive to you, it is likely to be attractive to somebody else—for example, the new incoming resident you're going to sell the house to when your residency is over.

Interviewing

This is the part of the process that applicants say makes them the most nervous. If you are competitive in other aspects of your application, then good interviewing skills can help you seal the deal. If some other part of your application is marginal, you may be able to make up all or part of that deficiency with an outstanding personal impression. The interview process is a two-way street, however. Be sure to use the time you have during your interview at a training program to learn all you can about the faculty, residents, training, and town.

19 Keep a journal

Keeping a journal is a great idea at any time in your life. Your interview trips are a time unlike any other in your life, and you will find it very interesting to record your thoughts, stories, feelings, and follies during this time. Not only will you have something to reflect on a few years down the road, but you will also be able to look back over your journal as you are ranking programs. This might be useful if you were having a bad day for some outside reason and the surrounding events colored your view of a particular program. The following tips that deal with housekeeping details during the interview process are really about what separates someone with a professional attitude and approach from someone merely hopeful they will get a residency spot.

20 Make notes about a program on the day you interview there

Even if you choose not to keep a journal about yourself during the interview process, you *must* write down notes about the programs and hospitals on the same day that you visit them. There will be many, many times when this is the last thing you want to do, but notes are critically important if you are interviewing at more than a handful of places. Just force yourself to do it while you are riding back to the airport or in the plane. If you are driving, attach a small voice recorder to your dashboard to record your thoughts as you drive. You can type these recordings up when you get home, but get your thoughts down in some manner on the same day as your interview. What you want at the end of the process is to be able to go back and review fresh and accurate remembrances of the programs you visited.

21 Add physical descriptors to the notes to help you keep everything straight

Don't forget to add some descriptions of physical features of the hospitals and programs. Making notes about the cases the residents see, the call schedule, and the staff is easy, but don't forget to include some of the unique things you saw while you were there. As crazy as it sounds, recording an odd color of carpet or an unusual exam room layout may be just enough to jog your memory and help you keep all the programs straight. It is not unheard of to have residents show up for the first day of work and realize that they confused the layout of the hospital for someplace else they had interviewed.

22 Handwrite personal thank-you notes

The number of residency applicants who fail to write any sort of thank-you note to the faculty and residents who interviewed them is simply unbelievable. This year's interview cycle just ended and I would estimate that I received notes from less than 20 percent of the candidates I interviewed. While it is certainly true that the applicants bear the expense and inconvenience of traveling to the program to interview, it is also true that every good program will interview many more applicants than it can take. With this in mind, you need to do everything you can to keep your name in the minds of the people who will be making the decision about which applicants get picked. Understand that the meeting to decide which applicants will be chosen may happen very quickly after you have interviewed. Many programs schedule these meetings within a few days to help them keep the applicants straight. So it should go without saying that a thank-you note that arrives a month after your interview is not going to do much good. Try to get your thank-you notes out within twenty-four to forty-eight hours after your interview.

Another real faux pas is to send a group thank-you note to each staff member you interviewed with, or to e-mail a thank-you note to the department chair or program director and copy the staff. It really only takes a few seconds to produce a unique handwritten note of two or three sentences, which is exactly what you should send to each and every staff person, chief resident, and administrative assistant you spoke with during the interview.

23 If faculty members suggest that you can call them with questions, find a question to call them about after your interview

Similar to the thank-you notes, this is an invitation to keep your name in front of the people who will be making the decision about which applicants get selected for the program you want. You should not waste the faculty's time with pestering phone calls, but after you have spent the entire day at a program, you should also be able to come up with one more legitimate question you could ask the staff. If a faculty member offers that you should call them if you have any more questions, take them up on the offer. Again, remember that decisions can be made very quickly after your interview, regardless of the actual date the list is due to the matching service. If you have a question to ask, call them soon after you leave (like the next business day).

24 Be honest with the people who interview you

There are two reasons to be honest. The first is that it is simply the right thing to do. The second is that physicians and their support staff are very good at picking up on the vibes when someone is trying to snow them. If they think they can't trust what you are saying, you will not get offered a spot no matter what kind of academic credentials you have. Also, if you spin a different story to each staff member you interview with, you will likely be caught when they all get together to discuss the candidates. At that point you will not be there to defend yourself and they will, in all likelihood, just move on to someone they think they can trust. In my experience, most of the urban legends students hear about someone with top-notch academics failing to match really means that they had problems in the area of honesty.

25 There is no "off the record" when you are interviewing

Just like they say on the TV show *COPS*, anything you say can and will be used against you. Or at least that is a fairly safe rule to live by while you are out on the interview trail. You may find yourself at any number of social functions with the residents or staff, and just because everyone is physically out of the hospital, that doesn't necessarily mean the interview process is over. Before you tell a questionable joke or bare your soul about your radical beliefs, you should take a moment and ask yourself how what you are about to say would stack up against just staying quiet.

26 Direct the appropriate questions to the appropriate people

It doesn't make sense to ask the chair of the department what resident in-house call is like, nor does it make sense to ask the junior resident in the program what the five- and ten-year goals of the department are. Both of these are good, fair questions but only if they are asked of the right people. Tailor your questions to the person you are talking to, but always have some questions to ask everyone you speak with.

27 Try to talk to residents at all levels

Just like before when I advised you to get information on different programs from people at different levels of practice and training, the same strategy goes for getting information about an individual program during your interview. Everyone will have a little different slant on what is going on within a given program and no one will likely be totally right or totally wrong. What you are looking for is not a single opinion in this process, but a trend of opinions one way or the other. If three or four people at different levels in a given program are telling you something (either good or bad), you should pay attention to what they are saying.

Conversely, an isolated negative comment from an individual staff member or resident that is not supported by similar comments from others probably doesn't deserve a lot of weight in your decision process. Everyone can have a bad day and some people (both staff and residents) are just generally negative about almost everything.

28

Have preplanned questions for the people who are interviewing you

Not having any questions to ask at all could be interpreted as not caring much about the program or just not being sharp enough to ask questions. You don't want either of these to be how you are remembered. "Where do you see yourself in five or ten years?" is a fair, inoffensive question for just about anyone you would meet during an interview. For the staff, this is a fair question for you to ask because you would want to know if they are still going to be there to participate in your education. For the residents, the answer to this question will tell you what the residents really plan on doing after they graduate.

29

Know some things about the people who are likely to be interviewing you (i.e., who the faculty and residents are at a particular program)

You should never just show up for an interview. In this age of technology, you should know the names of and something about everyone you are likely to meet prior to actually arriving at the program for the interview. Most programs have some sort of Web site and most professional specialty organizations have Web site listings of their specialists in a given geographical area. Basically, there is just no longer any reasonable excuse to show up at an interview uninformed if you are genuinely interested in that program.

30 Use an on-line database search to find out about all the papers each faculty member and resident has written

Once you know the staff names (and maybe the residents' names as well) it is relatively easy to go on-line and use a search service to see what each of them has published. I can absolutely tell you that if you do this, you will put yourself in a very small minority within the group of people who interview for a residency spot. Human nature being what it is, you will find that the people interviewing you will enjoy talking about themselves and what they have published. You will have also shown that you are able to gather information in an organized manner and that you are truly interested in that particular program. Both of these are considered excellent traits in a resident for any program. If you do not have much experience doing these types of searches, a reference librarian at your school should be able to help you. Also, your school likely subscribes to search services that may yield more data than you could get on your own.

31 Use the Web to find out which state, regional, and national offices the faculty holds

As mentioned in a prior tip, once you have the names of the people in the department where you will be interviewing, you can quickly find out which professional organizations they are active in and which offices they hold. Again, most people will enjoy talking about this type of activity with you, and you will again have demonstrated that you are interested in that particular field of medicine and have an above-average ability to find and organize useful information. This will give you another pleasant avenue of conversation during your interview time and help guard against the dreaded pregnant pauses during your conversations with the staff.

32 If possible, use some time the night before to walk through the area where the interview will take place

If you are traveling out of town for an interview, you will likely arrive in town the night before your interview. If you are staying close to the hospital where you will be interviewing, you might want to think about going over there in advance of the arranged time to get a feeling for the layout. You can find the clinic or offices where you will be interviewing and also get some sense of what the hospital is like at night, which in various places can be much different than it is during the day. In any event, for a small investment of time and effort, you will significantly decrease your anxiety on the day you actually interview. This is also just one more method to educate yourself about the program and to come up with intelligent questions during your interview the next day.

33

If you have an extra day, ask if you can round with the residents on the day that you are not interviewing

If you are staying overnight following your interview, you might consider asking if you can go on morning rounds with the residents the next day. This is a great chance to see the program in its native state. Once you are out of the formal interview situation, you will be able to see if the staff really is actively involved with the residents and how comfortable the residents are in their dealings with the faculty. Also, this is an excellent chance to see how the residents interact among themselves. Doing this also shows a real interest in the program.

34

Think before accepting coffee or soda if it is offered during the interview

At many interviews, you may be asked if you would like a soda or some coffee. Before you accept this, you might want to consider that most of these drinks will have caffeine and caffeine is a diuretic. As nervous as you are during an interview, you will be in worse shape if you need to use the restroom. Also, you can't spill something on yourself from a drink you don't have.

35 Say something positive in the interview that sets you apart as a person

Some programs will interview dozens of candidates a day during their interviewing process. Sometimes, the vote on the applicants will not happen until several days or even weeks after you have interviewed. With the staff meeting that many people, it is crucial that you give them something to remember that will set you apart as a person. This can be something relevant to the specialty you are considering, your education/experience, or just something unique about you as a person. Exact details are not important as long as they create a lasting positive memory of you. Prior to your interview, think of several uniquely positive things you could say about yourself. Once you have your list, try them out on some of your friends and get some feedback on the impression they create.

36 Have some idea about what you would like to do after residency, even if it is only a decision between academics and private practice

Most programs won't expect you to have your entire future planned out in exquisite detail. However, they will probably expect you to have at least a basic idea of what you will be doing in five to ten years. At a minimum, you should probably have an idea about whether or not you are planning a career in academic medicine. Of course, if you are fairly certain that you have a plan that seems right for you, you can go ahead and talk about it if you are asked what your plans for the future are.

37 Depending upon the program, some answers about your future practice may be more right than others

Different programs have different reputations and track records of the type of physician they produce. Some programs may see themselves as a training program almost exclusively for academic physicians. Other places may see their mission as turning out physicians practicing top-notch clinical medicine. Some programs may be a mix of the two, but usually one or the other will predominate. The easiest way to deduce what a program really does is to find out what the graduates have done for the last five years or so.

Realize, though, that the mission of a program can change with changing leadership. Don't blindly assume that just because the residents have all gone into clinical private practice for the last ten years that this is what the staff wants to keep happening. Be honest with yourself and your answers, because your real goal is not just to get into any program but also to find a program that will train you for what you want to do.

38

Have some answers prepared for off-the-wall questions

Because the interview process is long, repetitive, and tiring for the staff doing the interviews as well as for the applicants, you might find that some of the people interviewing you will throw out questions just to liven things up a little. Sometimes these questions may be used to see if you can think on your feet and if you have a sense of humor. Generally, if you have some relatively short, pat answer ready and then just sit there in silence, the interviewer will move on. If you truly don't know the answer to a question someone is asking you, another acceptable response is to simply answer, "I honestly don't know."

39

Have some answers prepared for offensive questions

In the worst of situations, these off-the-wall questions can be offensive and potentially illegal, but you are probably not in the best position to fight that battle during your interview trip. Generally, questions of this type are asked to try to get a reaction from you or to rattle you. Short answers —"yes," "no," and "I don't know"—are the best ones to fall back on in these situations. Once it becomes clear that you don't want to play that game, the interviewer will usually just go on to something else. Considering whether or not you would want to find yourself in a training program with the type of people who would behave in this fashion is extremely worthwhile. Rather than make a scene right then, you might want to just finish going through the motions of the interview and then quietly cross the program off your list as you are leaving the hospital. Although treatment such as this is not right or fair, the practical reality is that you are not in a position to affect much change at this point in your life. If you find yourself in this situation, consider that the silver lining in the cloud is that you found out early in the process that you would be better off somewhere else.

40 Use items in the interviewer's office to generate discussion during the interview

You should never have a problem finding things to talk about with your interviewer if the conversation is taking place in the interviewer's office. Look around for pictures of family, dogs, vacations, and other conversation topics. Look for books, both professional texts and popular titles. Look for sports equipment, running shoes, rackets, or other athletic items. Any of these things can be used as an icebreaker to start a discussion that will let the interviewer tell you something about themself. Remember that everyone's favorite topic to talk about is their own life.

41 Dress appropriately for the interview

The best advice for this is to think about what the president of the United States was wearing the last time you watched him on TV. What color was his suit? What color was his tie?

You probably can't remember these details and that is exactly the point. The idea was for you to remember the message, not the package. He probably wore a conservative dark suit and a conservative shirt and tie. The president does not want his clothing to detract from what he is saying, and you want exactly the same thing during your interview. The designer suit that cost thousands of dollars, the expensive jewelry, the expensive watch, and the expensive shoes may not make the impression you intended in this situation. While you don't want to show up in rags, you should aim for a happy medium of well-fitting clothes and accessories that are reasonably within the budget of a medical student soon-to-be resident. I can assure you from personal experience that if the staff members of a program remember you because of what you were wearing, then 99 percent of the time this will work against you.

42

Pack clothing appropriate for an interview and always bring an extra shirt, tie, or blouse in case of a spill or garment malfunction (See also tip 82)

Almost every year I have interviewed resident applicants, at least one of them has flown thousands of miles for the opportunity to interview in jeans and an old shirt. While the staff may feel sorry for someone like this and cut him or her some slack, noticing that your attire is far too casual will add to your nervousness and self-consciousness in an already stressful situation. You just don't need this kind of added pressure because it is so easy to avoid. Simply include the clothes you are going to interview in and one spare set of appropriate clothing as part of your carry-on luggage. Remember dark clothing shows spills and dirt much less than light-colored materials.

43

Always break in ahead of time the shoes you will wear while interviewing

This tip comes from personal experience. Many interviews will include a fair amount of walking during the day of the interview, so make sure that you are not wearing brand-new shoes. Blistered, bleeding feet will not add to your perfect interviewing state of mind. Likewise, some shoes are less comfortable by design (such as high heels) and may be difficult to wear all day even if they are broken in.

44 Build in breaks during the interviewing process

You may not have much control over the interview schedule, but all things being equal, building in some breaks is a good idea. This will keep you from going from one program to another until they all just become a blur. Probably doing a run of three to four programs and then taking a short break and then doing another three or four would be a pretty sensible and sane way to do it if you can. A break is not necessarily going back home. It may be spending time with your friends or members of your family for a few days just to decompress a bit from always having to be "on" during the interview process. If you are able to build in some breaks, this will help keep you fresh for the interviews later down the line.

Travel

Traveling to and from a residency interview is an expensive and time-consuming proposition. There is no known way to do this without spending any money; but after doing increasing amounts of business travel over the years, I have learned some tips that can make things easier and help cut down the bills. Some require flexibility and some may cost you a bit more in terms of time, but properly applied, these tips can be useful and workable ways to lessen the dent in your wallet.

The first thing to keep in mind is your travel plans should be as safe as possible. We all know that it may be possible to hitchhike from your home to a residency interview, but this would hardly be a wise idea for a number of reasons. However, there are many, many ways to reduce your travel costs without putting yourself at additional risk.

Depending upon your specialty choice, you may find that you are forced to fly to a number of interviews in distant cities, and this is where the costs can really add up. There are, however, good ways to keep your costs to a manageable level while still maintaining your sanity. Some of these ideas are not really tricks as much as just plain common sense.

45 Use a Saturday-night stay if it significantly affects the cost of your airline ticket

Saturday-night stays used to be almost a must with airline travel because ticket costs could literally triple (or more!) if you booked a round-trip flight that didn't include a Saturday-night stay. There has been some attempted movement away from this in recent years by some of the airlines, but checking the ticket cost with and without a Saturday-night stay is still worthwhile. Of course, the financial trade-off if you are staying Saturday night is buying a hotel room that in most cases you may not really need. Later on, we'll talk about ways to save money on hotels, and we will also discuss some methods of making it look like you are staying over Saturday night when you really might not. Obviously, the airlines frown on these techniques so they are presented for information-only purposes, and if you choose to use them, you also choose to accept all the risk and responsibility for whatever happens.

46 Fly from major hubs if you can

It is no secret that airlines price their tickets relative to the market pressure of the particular route that they are flying. Given this inescapable fact, it makes the most financial sense to book your flights from the major airline hub cities whenever you can, even if that means a bit of a drive. At this stage in your career, you may have more time than money, and if a major hub is within two to four hours from your home, you should also price tickets from that hub as well as the closest airport. After you have those figures, you can decide how much your time is worth per hour at this point in your life and see if it makes sense to drive to a larger airport.

47 Take advantage of special travel packages, Internet travel sites, and other offers (See also tip 49)

Airlines are continuously running specials. Usually these special fares are for routes that do not have the passenger load the airline would like to see or they may be for new routes the airline has just opened. The Internet has made finding these deals much easier, and you should always shop around the various travel Web sites to get an idea of what is currently available. There are also a number of Web sites set up by the airlines themselves as well as some third-party sites that will e-mail you a message about new promotions as they become available. For example, if you are interviewing in the mountain states in the late fall or winter, you should look at special ski fares the airlines sometimes offer. There is no rule that you actually have to ski, surf, or honeymoon (!) to take advantage of the advertised fares.

48

Make the most of frequent-flyer programs

There are really two aspects to the concept of frequent-flyer miles. The first is obtaining someone else's miles to use for yourself and the second is to get your own. In years past, there was a brisk business in the buying and selling of frequent-flyer miles. The airlines warned that they would refuse to honor any ticket purchased in this fashion, but in reality the rules for the transfer of miles were so lax that it was very uncommon to hear of anyone who was caught and punished.

However, now with increased security and the fact that all airlines and airports require a picture ID to get on the plane, the market for frequent-flyer miles seems to have slowed to a trickle at best. If your picture ID does not match the name on the ticket (never a problem in the past), the airline will not give you a seat. (Not to mention the fact that you may have some difficult explaining to do.) This restriction alone has curtailed the majority of transactions involving miles that are bought and sold.

At this point, some airlines will still allow members of the same family to use the miles, but you have to check carefully. It is always better to deal directly with the airline if you are trying to do this. Be sure to write down names, times, and locations of people you talk to on the phone, so if you show up at the airport and the counter person is refusing to issue you a seat, you will have some facts to back up what you are trying to do.

Since you can always use your own frequent-flyer miles, it goes without saying that you should *never* get on a flight without being a member of the airline's frequent-flyer program. Even if you think you won't be flying that much, you should still join the plan for any airline you may ever possibly use. Ideally, you should do this far enough in advance of your first flight on that airline so you will have your frequent-flyer card in hand when you check in. Getting credit for your flight is much easier if your mileage account number can be entered at the time you purchase your ticket or begin your flight. If you fail to do this, you may have to send in copies of your ticket after you get home to receive full credit for the miles you have flown. There are always delays when doing this, however, and you may have to do it more than once to get proper credit. It is just easier and more reliable to get the miles recorded at the actual time you fly.

A final way of accumulating frequent-flyer miles is to use an affinity credit card for one of the airlines. All of the airlines and many financial institutions have literally dozens of these types of deals available, and if you are currently using a credit card that does not give you any kind of perk, you should consider changing immediately. The trick to quickly building up miles in this way is to use your card for almost every purchase that you make — groceries, meals, clothes, and even small purchases that you used to pay cash for. For most of these cards, each dollar that you spend will get you credit for at least one mile in the frequent-flyer program. Some of these cards are better deals than others, and frequently if you inform a card issuer that you can get a better deal elsewhere, they will match or even beat the other deal if you have been a good customer.

Search the Internet using the keywords "frequent-flyer miles," "credit card," and "affinity card" for the up-to-date deals. There are many cards available with no annual fee that will give you one mile per dollar charged. I personally use a card with a small annual fee (less than fifty dollars) that gives me two miles for every dollar I charge. The miles are also good on any airline.

49 Use the Internet for airline information

Using a travel agent will add some cost to your airline ticket. Whether or not the extra cost is worthwhile is an individual decision and some of the following tips will explore this more fully (see tip 51 and following). The Internet now lets you do things you previously had to pay a travel agent to do, and there are dozens of Web sites that are available to help you find the best combination of flight times and price for your interviews. You can use any search engine (www.google.com, for example), type in "travel" or "airline reservations" and get many individual sites. Be aware, though, that many of the so-called independent sites are owned by the airlines. These sites may try to direct you to a particular airline or particular connections. This can be as subtle as how the order of flight choices is displayed and which airlines/flights are listed first. If you are booking your tickets yourself, you should always check several sites to try and find the best deal. If you choose to use an on-line travel site, find out if they have an emergency number to call if you have travel problems (see tip 51).

50 Know not only what flight you are taking, but what the alternates are

Use the on-line airline trip planners to get your itinerary and also to get alternate flights between the airports you will be using. Print this information and take it with you when you travel. Having this information physically with you and available can be a very powerful negotiating tool if your flight is cancelled and the airline is reluctant to book you on another airline's flight. If you know exactly what is available and the flight times, you will *dramatically* increase your leverage in dealing with the airline personnel at the counter. On several occasions, I have had them abruptly change their minds and agree to re-book me once they saw that I had essentially the same information about available flights as they did on their computer screen. Even on occasions when I have forgotten to do this, I have been able to sometimes bluff my way onto a new flight by just pulling out some papers and flipping through them while mumbling, "Doesn't airline X have a flight that leaves for there in an hour or so?"

51

Decide if you want to make your own reservations or use a travel agent

There are times when using a travel agent can be really helpful. First, agents will generally have more experience than you in booking flights. Even with the on-line reservation services available, in most cases they will have an interface that is quicker and easier to use. Perhaps the best reason to use a travel agent is that they will have an emergency number you can call if you miss your flight or it gets cancelled.

With this emergency number, you can use your cell phone while standing in line at the airport and get re-booked over the phone. By doing this, you can virtually move to the front of the line at the ticket counter or customer service desk. If you are already through the security checkpoint, you can just go directly to the gate your new flight is departing from and get your boarding pass issued there. If you are not through security, you will have to wait in line at the ticket counter to get your boarding pass because you will need your boarding pass to get through security screening. Although you will still be in line, your trusty travel agent will have already blocked a seat for you, and relief is a great feeling to have when something happens and the flights start to get messed up.

If you book your tickets on-line, you may not be able to hook up your laptop at the airport (if you even have it with you) and do the same thing as quickly when time really counts. Remember, at times like this the remaining available flights are rapidly filling with people

trying to do the same thing you are. Most travel agents
do charge a processing fee on tickets, but at times like
these the fee can seem like cheap insurance if you really need help getting somewhere.

52 If you use travel agents, be nice to them

Most people would be surprised how far a
little token of appreciation can go. If a travel
agent does something nice for you (or, in the beginning,
just does something routine for you), think about send-
ing a card, small flower arrangement, or other token
of your appreciation. Most of the time it seems like
people don't even say "thank you" anymore, and if you
go out of your way just a little, you will almost always
improve the service you get in the future. Make sure to
let the travel agent know that you are interviewing for
a residency and how important it is that you get where
you need to be on time. If you get them involved in the
process, you might be surprised at what they can do.
Just remember to include them on your list of people to
thank once you are successfully matched!

53 Ask the travel agent to keep checking for lower fares

Most travel agents will keep an eye out for
lower fares if you do more than occasional
business with them. Almost all of them have auto-

mated programs that will alert them if a fare is lowered because of a particular promotion. It also doesn't hurt to call and check on the fare status for your trip, particularly if you have booked the tickets several weeks to a couple of months before you are actually going to leave.

There are also Web sites that will alert you if a lower fare becomes available. However, you have to have access to your e-mail to be able to check these reminders and remember to check regularly.

54 Never take the last flight of the day

As I am writing this, I am actually sitting in an airport turning around to go home because I can't make an important meeting scheduled for tomorrow. My flight tonight (the last one out) is delayed and I will miss my connection (also the last flight out), so there is no way I can get to the meeting tomorrow morning. Under the heading of "do what I say, not what I do . . ." is my advice not to take the last flight out. If something goes wrong, there is no way to recover in time to make your appointment the next morning (and I am living proof of that right now)!

55

If possible, avoid the first of two flights close together to the same location (especially if your arrival time is critical)

If the first flight is lightly booked, the airline may co-incidentally have mechanical or other problems with the aircraft and shift all passengers over to the second flight. Frequently this flight will get in soon enough after the scheduled arrival of the first flight that the airline will not have to pay compensation, but it may be late enough compared to your original booking causing you to miss your connection or other transportation to your interview. The airlines will deny they do this, but if you talk to anyone who travels frequently, you will find that this type of rescheduling seems to happen more frequently than can be ascribed to random chance. This also seems to happen much more with flights with less passenger traffic.

56

Be on the lookout for overbooked flights

An overbooked flight can either be a headache or a gift horse, depending upon your situation. If you get bumped from a flight, you have rights to compensation, but if you miss your interview, the compensation the airline is required to give you is peanuts compared to what you have potentially lost by missing the interview (see following tip for suggestions on how to get what the airlines owe you). On the other hand, if you have built some flexibility into your schedule, you may voluntarily surrender your ticket and get some free flight vouchers for future trips. In this case, you are out some time, but if you have a lot of flying to do and funds are tight, this is a possible way to get some relief. Certain flights are chronically over-booked (again, a travel agent should be able to help with this), but if you are willing to take the risk of your flight being overbooked, you may come out a winner. In these situations, always identify yourself at the gate as someone who is willing to be bumped. Also, you will have to figure out what compensation you are willing to accept and see if the airline will meet that figure. As departure time approaches, the airline will invari-ably increase their offer if they still have a problem, but there will also be other people who will step up for the increased compensation.

57 Negotiate the stipend you receive if you voluntarily give up your ticket

There are no solid rules about these situ-ations, but the more experience you have with them, the better deal you will likely get. Always remember that you can counter the airline's offer. "We're offering three hundred dollars in flight coupons to anyone will-ing to be bumped from this flight" can be answered with "I'd be willing to be bumped for four hundred dol-lars" (or any other figure you think you can get). I have seen compensation amounts vary by hundreds of dollars depending upon how oversold the flight is and the anger level of the passengers in the gate area. Again, though, it is important to realize that as the compensation amount goes up, so will the number of passengers willing to take it. The airline does not have to pay everyone who volunteers, but rather will pay just enough people to solve their problem. Possibly, you may volunteer, not get any compensation, and have to take the flight as scheduled.

58 If at all possible, try to use one airline for the majority of your travel

Although the airlines have increased the number of miles you need for membership in the elite levels of their frequent-flyer clubs, they will also sometimes grant you membership for flying a certain number of segments. Depending on how often you fly and how many connections you make, you may qualify on the basis of the number of segments you have flown rather than the actual miles.

If you do qualify for the elite level in an airline's frequent-flyer program, they won't give you your own plane, but they will usually let you board first (when there is more room in the overhead storage for carry-on luggage). They may also send you upgrades and other perks that will not make flying free, but may make it a little easier. Anything that allows you to arrive at your interview better rested or in a better frame of mind will give you an advantage. Finally, if you qualify for elite status in one airline's program, another airline may grant you equivalent status in their program for a year if you ask them.

59 Pay attention to baggage rules

Different airlines have different rules for carry-on and checked luggage. The rules can apply to the number of pieces you are allowed to carry on and what sizes of luggage are allowed. This is made even more complex because of the variety of aircrafts currently in use.

Many smaller regional jets have very limited (briefcase or small backpack) overhead storage, but these flights will gate check your luggage. This means you leave your bag at the end of the Jetway as you board the airplane, and the airline delivers the bag back to the Jetway when you land. This process is more secure than regularly checking bags — your bag only has to go from the Jetway to the plane and back to the arrival Jetway—but the bag is still out of your physical control for a bit. I have never personally lost a bag in this process, but I also never gate check a bag with something fragile (like a laptop) inside.

Larger, regular-size airliners have more overhead space, but they will not gate check bags on those flights if the onboard storage is full. If you are among the last to board the plane and your bags won't fit under the seat ahead of you or overhead, they will check your carry-on bags with the regular checked bags to your final destination. In most cases, though, the airlines' liability on lost or damaged bags will be less on bags checked in this manner. The main thing is to know what kind of planes you will be on and have the right number and right size of carry-on bags so you can just keep going.

You also need to be aware that there are ever-changing regulations about which gels, liquids, batteries, chemicals, and other products can be carried on or even checked in an airplane. The most up-to-date information on current regulations can be found on the individual airline sites or on the Web site of the Transportation Security Administration (TSA).

60 Pick an aisle seat for long flights and a window seat for shorter flights

Where you sit is a personal preference, but I prefer to sit on the aisle if the flight is over three hours long and by the window if the flight is shorter. The aisle seat has the advantage of allowing you to get up and move around without disturbing anyone, but you will also have people (and the service cart) bumping into you and waking you up if you are trying to sleep. The window seat offers some protection from the aisle traffic, but the seat is harder to get out of if you need to stretch or use the restroom. Either seat is better than the middle, though.

The seat at the front of a seating section is called the bulkhead seat. Some people prefer this seat because there is generally more leg room. However, I personally try to avoid these seats because there is no under-seat storage in front of you and these seats are also attractive to people traveling with small children. This is because the kids can move around and still be under control without crawling all over the back of someone's seat in front of them.

Now, my medical practice is about 90 percent kids and I love kids, but having been the unwilling recipient of several milk and cookie showers while in a bulkhead seat, I generally opt to sit someplace else.

61 Book an aisle and a window seat if you are traveling with a companion

If there are two of you traveling together, try to book a window and an aisle seat in the same row. Since nobody wants to sit in the middle seat, there is a chance the middle seat between you will remain open if the flight is not sold out. Even if someone shows up with a ticket for that seat, they will almost always trade you for either the window or the aisle so you and your traveling companion can sit together.

62

Consider buying back-to-back tickets

Right up front, let me say that this information is presented for informational purposes only because the airlines have said they will punish anyone they catch doing this by voiding the ticket and taking back frequent-flyer miles. I am personally unaware of anyone who this has happened to, but that certainly does not mean it has not happened. As mentioned before, with increasing security it is probable that the airlines will use computer tracking to identify individuals who routinely use these practices.

Basically, the practice of booking back-to-back tickets involves buying two separate tickets for one round-trip flight where both of the tickets involve a Saturday-night stay or other type of discount. As you are certainly aware if you have flown much at all, two people rarely pay the same price for tickets on the same flight, and various discounts can dramatically reduce the cost of your ticket. This fact is why you can sometimes buy two discounted tickets and still save considerable money compared to buying a single ticket without a discount. Each ticket contains one part of your intended flight and your plan is to use half of each of the two tickets. For example, ticket "A" contains your outbound flight and you don't care which return is booked (as long as the ticket qualifies you for the discount you are seeking and you get the fare break).

Ticket "B" contains your return flight, again with the second part of the ticket to occur on any day so you qualify for the discount and get the fare break on that ticket also. *Both* the outbound and return legs on the respective tickets must be the *first* segment on that ticket. If they are not and you do not show up for the first segment, the airline will void the return segment and your ticket will be worthless.

Again, all airlines have publicly said that they take a very dim view of this or any of the other "gray-area" booking schemes presented. You can battle with them if you like, but if you really need to get somewhere and they tell you that they are going to void your ticket, you are going to be stuck. Also realize that some travel agents will refuse to knowingly book tickets in this fashion. You have to decide how much risk you are comfortable taking and what your options are if the airlines get tough with you.

63 Consider buying hidden-city tickets

This is another gray area as far as the airlines are concerned. Some flights that connect through or lay over in a given city are much cheaper than a direct flight to that particular town. The way this discrepancy can be utilized is to buy a ticket for the connecting flight and just get off at the intermediate stop (which happens to be your desired destination) and not continue on to where your ticket says you were planning to go. Obviously, this will only work if you have carry-on luggage. Again, this information is presented for educational purposes only. The airlines claim they are computer tracking this practice now, and if they catch you doing this or anything else they consider illegal, they will void your entire ticket.

64 Consider traveling to alternate airports

This is totally legitimate and should be a consideration every time you fly. In some major metropolitan areas around the country, there may be more than one airport with frequent service to a given geographical location. For example, in New York City you could choose from Kennedy, LaGuardia, or Newark, NJ, and in Washington, D.C., you could choose from Reagan, Dulles, or Baltimore. Flights into some of these airports may be significantly cheaper than others and if you are on a tight budget, the extra time and cost for a ground shuttle may be more than offset by what you save on the airline ticket. You want to be sure that you understand what is involved with getting from the airport to the city you are traveling to and what additional expenses you will incur in getting there and back to the airport before you book the flight. An excellent book about ground transportation from airports all over the world is Salk International's *Airport Transit Guide.*

65 Get to the airport early

There is an old saying that the person with the most flexibility in any situation will always win and airline travel is no exception. The earlier you get to the airport, the more choices you will have if the flight is cancelled and the more likely the counter agents are to be cooperative. There are obviously limits to how early you can get there, but if I have the choice of having to sit in one place or another, I will usually head to the airport. Having a little extra time can keep an unexpected delay from becoming more than just an inconvenience. There are enough stressors during the interview process and being in a position to be flexible if scheduled flights change is one factor you can control. Less stress always equals a better performance during your interview.

66 Make sure your bags are checked through to the correct final destination

Do not leave the ticket counter until you have your baggage receipts. These are small slips of paper with a UPC bar code on them that the agent will staple to your ticket jacket. Make sure you have one of them for each bag you checked and that each of them has the correct final destination. Make sure you hang on to these baggage receipts until your checked bags are back in your hands at the baggage carousel. In some airports you will need to show them to a security guard to get out of the baggage claim area.

67 Get from the plane to the baggage carousel as quickly as possible

Cat Stevens was right when he sang his hit "Wild World"—it *is* a wild, wild world out there. In every airport, there are people who will try to take advantage of travelers who are away from home. It goes without saying that you have to keep an eye on your stuff and a bag that just keeps going around and around on the carousel is pretty tempting for a thief, especially if there is no one around looking for it. I usually tell myself that I will have plenty of time to look at whatever airport shops look attractive on my way home and beat it down to baggage claim to grab my bag before someone else does. I also have small but distinctive tags or straps on my bag so I can immediately identify it as soon as it comes out on the baggage belt.

68 Protect yourself from theft in airports

It is an unfortunate fact of life that theft occurs all around us. Certainly an airport is no exception, and there are several reasons why your risk may go way up when you travel. When you are in an airport, you are in a strange environment and you are preoccupied with a number of things, including how to get to your gate, where you left your car, where to check your bags, and on and on. Also, you are in an environment where there are a lot of people moving around you quickly and bumping into you. Finally, you are likely to be carrying cash, credit cards, or other personal belongings with a significant value.

Obviously there is not one specific way to prevent becoming a victim of theft, but there are ways to reduce your risk. Be aware of your surroundings, put your valuables where they are secure and inaccessible to pickpockets, and always keep an eye on your carry-on bags. Many travel stores sell alarms and cable locks for carry-ons. Depending upon the contents of your carry-ons, you might want to consider these, but alarms and locks are no substitute for continued vigilance over your things.

69 Put your name and flight schedule inside your bags

Generally speaking, the airlines will not check your bag unless you have your name on a tag on the outside of it. This system works fine until the tag gets ripped off somewhere along the way and your bag becomes an orphan with no way to be reunited with you. Even if you and your bag get separated and the tag stays on, the bag will have your home address and your bags may be returned there while you are still on your trip. The airlines claim that before a bag is declared permanently lost and sold to companies specializing in lost freight (www.unclaimedbaggage.com), they will open the bag and try to find something identifying the owner. For this reason, I put a photocopy of my address and flight itinerary inside each bag I check. For longer trips, I also write my home address and the address of any hotels I know I will be in and the dates I will be there. This way there is at least a chance that if my bags and I become separated, I may get them back while I am still gone.

70 Lock your bags if possible

There are sporadic reports of theft from checked bags in the news lately. It seems that unscrupulous baggage handlers have opened bags, quickly looked for something valuable, and then closed the bag again and moved on. The victim doesn't know anything is wrong until they get to the hotel, and by then it is almost impossible to prove that the theft occurred while the bag was under the care of the airline. The simple solution to this is to lock your bags. Currently this is more difficult to do because of heightened security at airports around the United States. Sometimes, if you are nice to the TSA personnel at the checked baggage screening station, they will lock your bag for you after the bag has gone through the screening machine. However, if you absolutely have to put something of value in your checked bags, at least put the valuable item in something so it is not obvious or easily accessible when the bag is quickly opened.

71 Use crummy luggage to check

I have never had great luggage but once when my wife and I were first married, we were checking into a flight at Kennedy Airport in New York City, and the agent commented on the fancy garment bag my wife had. "You'll never see that again if you check it," said the lady at the check-in counter. We appreciated the advice and carried the garment bag aboard. The bottom line is there is just no reason to increase your chances of theft by using new or expensive luggage which becomes a target simply for the luggage itself, regardless of what is inside. Buying less flashy or even used luggage can make a lot of sense. Most people don't think about this, but many second-hand stores, including the Salvation Army, have a decent selection of suitcases and bags. Don't worry about making an impression with your luggage when you are on the interview trail. If you make a good impression with yourself, no one will notice your luggage.

72 Put your carry-on bags where you can see them—in the bin across the aisle

Experts also say that some baggage theft occurs on the planes themselves when thieves grab items out of the overhead bins and disappear into the crowd. This type of crime is why it is important to put your belongings where you can see them, even on the plane. The best place to store your bags is in the overhead bin *across* the aisle from the row you are sit-

ting in. If you think about it, you really can't see your
bags if they are in the bin above your head, especially
if you are in a window seat. Once again, vigilance is
the best protection against theft, even if you are distracted by what you are going to be doing once you
get off the plane.

73

Make sure you read the departures screen and not the arrivals screen when you are connecting

This sounds too simple to ever happen which
means that it does, and it can happen to you (I still do
it sometimes when I am in a hurry). Obviously, you
want to head to the gate where your flight is *departing
to* your destination city, not *arriving from* it.

74

A good hotel is one that has free transportation to and from the airport

Surprisingly, you will frequently find that the
most expensive hotels do not always have the most
services. Mid-price-range hotels, however, are fiercely
competitive and often have to offer services other
than just a room to entice travelers to stay at that particular facility. When booking a hotel room, ask if the
hotel has free transportation to and from the airport.
Depending upon the city and the distance, you will
likely save between twenty and forty dollars in cab

fare each way. Ideally, the hotel will be closer to the hospital where you will be interviewing so that if you do ultimately need to take a cab, you will at least have a much shorter ride to pay for. Another way to use the free transportation is in the situation where the hotel is the wrong direction from the airport relative to the hospital where you will interview. In this situation, just take the free shuttle back to the airport and then catch a cab to the hospital. This will save you paying for a cab just to make up the distance back to the airport. In the unlikely situation that anyone would say anything about heading to the airport with no bags, you can just say you have a meeting at the airport and that should take care of it.

75 A better hotel is one that has free transportation to and from the airport and is close to the hospital where you will be interviewing

This is true for all the reasons outlined above and is especially true if the hotel is within walking distance of the hospital or offers free transportation to the hospital and back. It is important to consider that free airport transportation and walking distance (or free hospital transportation) is worth at least twenty to forty dollars, so even if you have to pay a little more for a room it would still be well worth the extra money.

76 The best hotel is one that has all of the above, free breakfast, and hors d'oeuvres during happy hour

By now it should be obvious that your goal is to pay for a room and get everything else for free. Many hotels now have a manager's reception in the late afternoon with free drinks and free food. Depending on the hotel property, this could easily serve as dinner in many circumstances. As you are comparison shopping for a hotel room, be sure to find out if they also offer a free happy hour in addition to free transportation. Expect to pay a little more than a comparable competitor (but still usually much less than a higher-end hotel), but be happy knowing that you will make it up by saving on transportation and meal costs. This is just one more way to turn the odds in your favor by arriving at your interview well rested and well fed.

77 Sacrifice a view for a room away from the elevators and ice machines

Depending on when you check in, your choice of rooms may be limited, but it never hurts to ask for exactly what you want and negotiate from there. Rooms at the end of the hall are usually quieter because they are away from the elevators and ice machines, and there are not a lot of people walking back and forth in front of your door. Traveling is stressful enough, even under the best of circumstances. There is just no substitute for a good night's sleep.

78

Know how to get out of the hotel in case of a fire

If you don't get anything else out of this book, please get this. *Everytime* you check into a hotel room, put your bags in the room and then walk back out in the hall and find the two fire escapes that you would use to get out of the hotel in case of a fire. Count the doors or other landmarks so you can find the right door by touch if necessary, because if the smoke is thick, you will not be able to see the exit door. If all this sounds like paranoia, consider that most experts agree that the major cause of death in hotel fires is that people have no idea how to get out and needlessly die in the confusion that follows.

79

Look for restaurants in the area around the hotel

The restaurants in hotels provide convenience, but this usually comes at a price. In every major city there are usually a number of restaurants around the hotel ranging from fast food to local favorites. Ask someone in the hotel if the area is safe to walk around before you go exploring, but this can also be a good chance to get a feel for the city where you are interviewing.

80

Ask the residents where to eat around the hospital and around where you are staying

After your interview, eating in the area around the hospital is especially convenient if that is possible and safe. If you ask the residents about this toward the end of your interview day, they will probably give you the lowdown on some local place to eat. After all, this is where they usually eat because they are probably sick of the food in the hospital, and they don't have the time or money to drive all over town. One or more of the residents may even join you and possibly give you a lift back to your hotel, thus saving another cab fare.

81

There is nothing wrong with carrying your own bags

I have a lot of sympathy for doormen and bellmen who work in hotels. They have a tough job. However, if money is very tight while you are interviewing, you will probably be better off eating with the money you would have used as a tip for someone handling your bags. There is nothing wrong with carrying your own bags in the hotel, and who knows, if the interviews work out you'll be in a position to make it up to them someday.

82

Use a wheeled bag to lighten the load

The smartest invention in luggage since the zipper was to put wheels on the bottom of it so the luggage doesn't have to be carried. Some of these types of bags have a strap that lets you piggyback additional luggage on them. I have owned one of these wheeled bags for years and it has made traveling a lot easier. I have found that the carry-on size of these seems to work the best because you can still use it to carry additional luggage, and you can also carry it on the plane with you. This might be a great place to have a spare clean shirt, dress, blazer, pair of pants, or shoes so if your checked luggage gets lost, you can still show up in something other than jeans.

83

Take along spot remover in your carry-on luggage

No matter how careful you are trying to be, you will get spots on your clothes. Following Murphy's Law, these will most likely be the clothes you are planning on interviewing in. Pack a little multi-purpose spot remover to rehabilitate your wardrobe while you are on the road.

84

Coordinate trips with students from your home institution

Use bulletin boards, listserves, broadcast e-mails, or other ways to connect with students at your local institution and try to find other applicants to split expenses with (even if they are interviewing in other specialties). Specific examples of ways to do this will be outlined in some of the tips that follow.

85

Make friends on the interview trail

Interviewing is a very stressful time. It is easy to feel that your entire future is riding on what happens in the few weeks you have set aside to interview at residency programs where you would like to go. However, you do not need to make yourself more miserable than necessary. You will meet many great people on the interview trail who have similar interests to yours.

Sure, it is true that you are, in some cases, competing with them, but it is also true that there are a lot of spots in every specialty. Quite possibly, many of the people you meet will get spots in programs you are not as interested in without knocking you out of the competition for programs you like. You will likely meet some of the same people again and again while you are interviewing at different programs. Take some time to get to know these folks. I have known of medical students who called up their new interviewing friends and used these contacts for housing, transportation, and food during their interview trips.

86 Offer housing to people interviewing at your program

In keeping with the above advice, if you can easily accommodate some applicants who are interviewing at your local program, you should give serious thought to doing so. Most of the people would be happy to reciprocate in some way. Having even one friend in a strange city can make all the difference when you visit that city to interview.

87 Consider splitting hotel room costs

If you get to know some of the applicants fairly well as you are going about interviewing at various locations, you might consider sharing upcoming hotel rooms if you are going to be at the same place at the same time. This is also a good option if several of you from your local medical school are going to be interviewing in the same city at the same time, even if you are interviewing for different programs. Generally, medical schools will have bulletin boards or listserves for such announcements and you should make use of them.

Again, remember that though it is hard to get over the competitiveness that plagues medical school, you are not necessarily competing for exactly the same spot with every other applicant. Different programs will appeal to different applicants for different reasons. It really is possible for many people to win in the interview process.

88 Connect with long-lost relatives and friends

This tip is all about killing two birds with one stone. You can actually have fun seeing relatives and friends that you haven't seen for some time while getting a free place to stay and eat. If you do end up in that city for your residency training, these same folks can be an invaluable resource when it comes to finding things such as a place to live, a vet for your pet, or someone to work on your car.

89 Connect with friends of long-lost relatives and friends

You have to decide how far out on the limbs of your relationship tree you want to climb, but if money is very, very tight, there is certainly nothing wrong with asking if your friends or relatives know of anyone who might help you out while you are in their town. The worst thing that can happen is you will strike out and end up no worse off than if you had not asked at all. Of course, you also have to weigh the risks of getting into a car or staying with someone you do not know well or at all.

90 Definitely share cabs to hotels

This can work to your advantage in several circumstances. If you are traveling with people you know or you recognize people on the plane, consider asking if they have a place to stay and if they would like to split the room costs or at least the cab costs to the hotel. Again, the worst that can happen is they will say no and you are no worse off than you would be if you hadn't asked.

The other way this can work is when you hear someone say where he or she is going while you are standing in line waiting for cabs at the airport. Keeping in mind that staying safe is the main thing, you may want to casually ask them if they would like to split the fare since you are going to the same place. Sometimes people will say no, but sometimes they will welcome the company just to have someone to talk to.

91 Use e-mail to keep in touch and save on phone bills

E-mail is the greatest invention for the traveler since the inn by the road. Very, very few things that you would have previously called someone about require an immediate answer, but you pay a relatively high cost for long-distance voice service. For messages that fall more under the "Hey, I'm alive" category, use your e-mail account as much as possible. There are ways to set up free Web-based e-mail accounts (hotmail.com is one that I have used), which allow you to check your e-mail from any computer with Internet access. Everyday, more cyber coffeehouses and Internet kiosks are popping up in both shopping districts and airports. Check the fee before using them, but if you are dealing with a batch of e-mails this can prove to be a very economical way to communicate. This also means that you may not always have to take a laptop along for the sole purpose of checking your e-mail.

92 A cell phone with a national access plan, plenty of minutes, e-mail, Internet, and texting capabilities may be a great investment at this time in your life

Being able to use your phone to check your e-mail, text someone, and access the Internet is a liberating feeling and can help relieve a lot of stress. You'll need to shop around to get the best deal, and you want to make sure you understand the terms of your agreement. Ideally, you are looking for a deal where you can add or subtract features on a monthly basis as your needs change while you are interviewing. These plans can become pretty pricey, but the ability to be connected anytime anywhere has real advantages during your residency application process.

As good as this technology is, though, don't forget to have a regular phone card with a good number of minutes available. Nothing beats a pay phone if your cell phone is broken, discharged, or stolen.

93 Always have at least two people who know where you are every day

After surviving the rigors of medical school, it may be tempting to take a break during your interview time and just drop off the face of the earth for a while. However, you are not quite home free yet. Until the authority governing your particular match receives your match lists, you need to be in a position where you can be reached quickly 24–7.

I think the best way to do this is to have a permanent phone number on record with the programs you are looking at, which will be answered by a live person while you are traveling. Most likely a commitment of this level will come from someone in your family. You will have to take responsibility to contact whoever agrees to do this at least once a day or more frequently if things are really hopping.

Closing Thoughts

So . . . things didn't work out the first time like you wanted them to. No one expects you to be happy about being in this position, but it is not the end of the world either. And not getting into a program the first time around definitely does not mean that you will never get the residency you want.

94

Play within the rules of the match, the first time and every time you apply

This tip is an extension of the previous discussion. If you start to look sleazy or dishonest, in any context, the majority of good programs will simply just move on to someone who *is* honest (or at least appears to be so). Almost everyone I have ever talked to would take the most honest applicant over the smartest. Most of the problems that residents encounter in their programs and with their faculty come from some form of dishonesty. The most intelligent applicant in the world will not be able to outsmart a perception of dishonesty.

95

Expect that the programs will play within the rules of the match

You have every right to expect that the programs you are applying to will adhere to the rules of the match. No one is naive enough to believe that all programs will do so, but the really good programs just have too much to lose by trying to circumvent the procedures in place. Just like with applicants, the reputation a program has can be quickly and very negatively impacted if word gets out that the program is dishonest with applicants.

96
Don't volunteer the fact that you are interviewing for a second time

Although some of the people interviewing you will likely remember you from the last time, it is possible that they may not. Don't take this personally. The staff interviewing you might have been very busy or distracted the last time they met you. You may have been part of a large number of resident applicants that they interviewed, or the people doing the interviewing this year may not have done it last year. This actually happens a lot in some programs where the duties of interviewing are passed around.

It is sad to say, but many of the people interviewing may not have spent much time reviewing your file prior to your interview, and if you don't volunteer the fact that you are interviewing for the second time, they may not even know. Of course, not volunteering information that may not help you is completely different from a situation in which you are directly asked if you failed to get into the program previously. This situation is covered in the next tip.

97
Be prepared to give reasons why you think you did not get in the first time around

Without doubt, someone will ask you why you think you didn't get into the program the first time. From a superficial viewpoint, this may seem like a mean question. However, this is probably a fair question to ask to see if you have any insight on what your weaknesses may have been and what you have done to correct the situation. There may be legitimate reasons that you didn't get in even though you were a good candidate.

Maybe you didn't apply to enough programs, maybe an unethical program director promised you a position and didn't deliver and you didn't leave other options open on the application, or maybe your C.V. was a little light on something that would have helped your application (publication of research, for example).

In any event, there are several, if not many, perfectly plausible reasons why you may have been an excellent candidate but didn't get in. So don't hang your head and mumble when someone asks you about this. Use the opportunity to emphasize why you are now a much better candidate than you were when you went through the process previously. Be sure to convey that you are not bitter about the process, but rather that you see it as a learning experience. Highlight the positive changes you have made to improve yourself and your application.

98 Get an honest second opinion about your application

What you are looking for here is someone who will be constructively blunt about your application. What you are not looking for is someone who will tell you the system is unfair, you were cheated, or not to worry—you'll get in next time. The system may be unfair, you may have been cheated, and I hope you do get in the second time, but none of that is really important at this point.

The process you are involved in is the only one that you are going to get, and you simply have to make the best of things as they are. You may have a chance to change the system later in your life, but first you are going to have to get in a position to do that. And that means you are going to have to work with the system that is in place now.

99 Get an honest opinion about your personality and how you come across to other people

This is the hardest of all the information to honestly get and it can be the hardest of all things to hear. That being said, this may absolutely be the key that unlocks your future dreams. Every year I interview people who are going to have a very tough time getting a spot even though they easily have the academic credentials to do anything they want. This can be because of arrogance, indifference, evasiveness, or just a vibe that something isn't right. Many, many times this is probably not the case, but with the limited interview time available, there just isn't time to be sure that this person isn't going to cause trouble.

I am also more certain with each passing year that some of these people have no idea how they come across to others. If you are having problems getting accepted into a program and you have excellent academic credentials and reference letters, consider getting an honest opinion about how you affect others when you interact with them. This may be from a close friend or a professional counselor, but the person has to be someone who has the capability of being objective. Your responsibility is not to get defensive and just listen to what you are being told. You really need to have no response at all at the time. Just listen. Then go off and think about what you learned and think about how you might want to change things to alter the effect that you are having.

100 Improve your application

If you don't get in on the first pass, you should take an objective look at both your application and how you come across, as outlined in the previous two tips. This should not be a process of beating yourself up about things you can't change (like first-year grades), but rather an objective look for things that you can add or improve to make yourself more competitive. All the things mentioned previously, which make an application strong (like research experience or publications), are more important than ever when you are repeating the application process.

If you don't have any of these, get some. If you have some, get more. Virtually anyone on staff in any field of academic medicine has several ideas for papers or case reports waiting to be written up that they just don't have time to do. With just a little effort, you should be able to find one or several things that will bolster your application.

101 The bonus

The bonus is easy. It is really only two points that deserve re-emphasis— don't give up and don't sell yourself short. Together, these two are unbeatable. If you have a dream, then there is nothing stopping you from trying to attain it but your own attitude and efforts. Your dream is, at the same time, both possible and impossible. Your success depends on your attitude and what you think you can do.

I have seen many people from every life circumstance imaginable get exactly what they want even in the face of seemingly overwhelming odds. You can do it too. And I hope some of these tips will help you do just that. Good luck!